SIXTY THOUSAND SILENT ANGELS

by Isaac Philo

2020–2025

This is a collection of poetry. Some subjects have been fictionalized to differing extents beyond the obvious fictionalization concomitant to the devices of figurative language. Many subjects are entirely metaphorical. This collection covers many sensitive themes; reader discretion is advised. Poems concerning sensitive themes are written from particular vantage points which are sometimes speculative and not necessarily the personal perspective of the author. Nothing in this book is intended or rightly interpreted as a threat to anyone.

Scripture quotations marked "Dar" are taken from the DARBY BIBLE, published in 1867, 1872, 1884, 1890; public domain.
Scripture quotations marked "WEBU" are taken from the WORLD ENGLISH BIBLE UPDATED, public domain. "World English Bible" is a trademark of eBible.org.

Cover design by Isaac Philo.

First edition, 2025.

ISBN: 979-8-218-62809-3 (Paperback)
ISBN: 979-8-218-59908-9 (Hardcover)

Published by Isaac Philo.

Dedicated to my parents, grandparents, brothers, sisters, writing club, all those whom I love, and especially—
to God above.

Preface

For five years, the strike of midnight has marked a fruitful hour. Some may call it the witching hour, but I have fought that infernal power, and it did not prevail. In wandering and hypnagogic ideation came reflections far truer to their sources than those which the critical and logical processes of midday usually allow. Concretized, now, in words of incontrovertible constancy, I captured the mind of midnight; the only remnants of its fleeing and intangible oneironicity are either the feelings the words evoke when read or the darkness of the ink itself.

For five years, I have daily approached an understanding of the word "katalambanō." Hailing from the Koine Greek of John 1:5, this word is variously translated as both "comprehended" and "overcome." I am no linguist, but neither am I a stranger to language. We have here one single word, encompassing both the concepts of triumphal struggle and understanding—as if the chaos of a world uncomprehended is defeated the moment we give it a name.

I have named the shadows and the sunlight, and they now both dwell, comprehended, in this book, my mind, and my heart. But I did not overcome the sunlight. Ten seconds staring at the sun will remind you of the ease of an open eye in shadows. No, *I* was overcome—by the light of the Word.

In the beginning was the Word. Let us not deify the written word—the reference. Let us, rather, turn our eyes to the Word of whom it speaks—the referent. The sum total of reality, though homogenous at the largest scales, points as sharply as any arrow in a single direction.

Isaac Philo,
January 2025

Contents

"Or do you think that I couldn't ask my Father, and he would even now send me more than twelve legions of angels?"

(Matthew 26:53 WEBU)

Chapter 1

Nightfall

4

"Their idols are silver and gold, the work of men's hands:
They have a mouth, and they speak not; eyes have they,
and they see not;
They have ears, and they hear not; a nose have they, and
they smell not;
They have hands, and they handle not; feet have they, and
they walk not; they give no sound through their throat.
They that make them are like unto them,—every one that
confideth in them."

(Psalms 115:4–8 Dar)

The Mirror

Somewhere,
in a faded and dusty corner of yesteryear's attention,
stands a mirror.

In an urban cove,
a gray mane
growing whiter in the bleach of the sun.

When the windowpane consents to transparency,
a slight glimmer flits a fitful path across the room
in microscopic proportions.

The slightest shimmer
of an orphaned synapse.

The windowpane
as active as the window frame,
as eager as the mirror's frame;
it speaks of the gaze of fame
still leaking
from a half-remembered glory.

Borne to the light of a brighter eye
as the image they thought was reflection;
enamored of the flesh that felt too familiar;
it was not flesh,
but it was the best a sleeping stone could do.

An undilated pupil shined a brighter iris
in the unrestricted umbra of the midday star.
A shadow cast on metacognition
in the heads of eyes held captive.

But the brightened border was a veneer,

and dusk laid bare the illumination due to the gilded
glass:
None at all.

Without a picture, no longer did they
grace the place that once traced their face.
In the desiccated soil that speckled that wordless space,
an adamantium silence blanketed the chilling surface
that had glowed with a crowd of onlookers.

What they had looked on, they had looked upon;
they were looked upon, but they knew not whom
they saw.

The crypt,
when closed,
chained a guiltless clasp across the anesthetic recollection
of the new moon.

No one cried for the thickening thoughtless sky—
the glass alone was darkened.

The day returned, and joy labored on,
incarnate.

Unhindered by the plight—
still laid the mirror,
inanimate,
in eternal night.

"Count it all joy, my brothers, when you fall into various temptations, knowing that the testing of your faith produces endurance. Let endurance have its perfect work, that you may be perfect and complete, lacking in nothing."

(James 1:2-4 WEBU)

Sisyphus

Sisyphus laid the rock at the hill's summit.
The day was done, and the tension fled from his
spine.
No more labor.
Finished.

So kind of you to come along!
Your mesa marks the sabbath.
The stability of the horizon
finds a home in your horizontal.
You alone
own the strength of the climb.

No.
Open your eyes, Sisyphus.

Sisyphus laid the rock against the incline.
45 degrees, neither up nor down.
The rock and the bone, and their calcified pact.
The one regresses
what the other progresses.
Rain falls towards the rising pressure.
The feet find their hold.

Does the boulder open its eyes?

Sisyphus chiseled away.
Chiseled at the climb? Yes.
Chiseled at the rock? No.
Chiseled himself?
Is he the rock?

Sisyphus has always been close to something,

always far from the end.
His efforts near,
his outcomes hazy, unclear.

But he was never far from himself.

But Sisyphus sat down,
with his eyes open.
His eyes *were* open.
What now could he not withstand?

And the bed of stone pushed up.

"I am counted among those who go down into the pit.
I am like a man who has no help,
set apart among the dead,
like the slain who lie in the grave,
whom you remember no more.
They are cut off from your hand."

(Psalms 88:4–5 WEBU)

Ravine

I stand at the foot of an icy ravine.
It rains.
It rains and I,
hypothermiated in the unabated chill,
gaze up the frozen walls.

Is there land up there?
Is this wall a wall dividing infinitely many equally
deep pits?
What beyond this sits?

Oh. There it is.
Degrees backward on the turning clock hands.
I now recall.

To slip and to fall, and
down, I then knew the wall,
and could not crawl or return whence I came.
I could not regain the frame.

I'm in the same crevice I met when,
once, as a menacing wafting fog,
the whipping tide of the wind gurgled the gas-masked
preppers.
They could not be ready;
calamity would not be downspoken in penetrating
capacity.

But the cold front cannot freeze the living water.
May I find my way out,
make my way to it.
May I drink life,
may I pierce the wind,
may I crack the ice.

May I carve a foothold,
another,
and every step of the vertical walkway.

May I melt the wailing onslaught,
warm the winds,
and win
an amiable ambiance.

I will close my eyes,
unvigilant.
I will not leave the allegiance of the air
ambivalent.

"But I am a worm, and no man;
a reproach of men, and despised by the people."

(Psalms 22:6 WEBU)

They still stand

I looked in the wrong direction.

My nails fall off my toes.
My toes fall off my feet.
My feet fall off of my legs.
My legs fall off of my waist.
My head falls off of my shoulders.
My brain falls out of my skull.

Rolling now,
crawling in the grimy dust,
re-forming where my gaze had terminated—
where I had terminated

But I did not know the brain that took my place.
Dried up like a worm somewhere on the parched
concrete,
I was not the man that rose again.

He stares at me, scoffs, and streaks my axons against
the asphalt.
It takes little, quite little, when strength asserts itself
in that stature, with its arm around her figure.

That figure.

"He hurls down his hail like pebbles.
Who can stand before his cold?"

(Psalms 147:17 WEBU)

can't

Warm
It's not
That's not the way
It is, it's cold
It's clammy, shaking
Shivers of the kind that aren't
Shivers but the thought of how I
Wish to wither without waking
Pray the Lord my soul is taking
Tunnel, circles black the lighthouse
The tunnel I'm already past
The lighthouse had to take a break
My sky once more as a tunnel cast
When bright white spectra full of greatness
Surrender what they truly are
And lighthouse lights shine absent lumens
And shine so dark they put out stars
I followed what I thought would guide me
I met the lighthouse with intention
But force of will can only move you
Never removes your hope's suspension
Untenable promises I had promised
And promised to myself, at that
But with these useless eyes, in darkness
Bad news, and I'm the diplomat
To me, praying a good reaction
But I'm without an alternate
Not hoping for it all at once
I'd hoped for one
I needed one
And I got none
And I can't

"Now the serpent was more subtle than any animal of the field which the LORD God had made. He said to the woman, "Has God really said, 'You shall not eat of any tree of the garden'?""

(Genesis 3:1 WEBU)

The Basilisk

Pupils in the ground-up concrete:
Manufactured eyes
Basilisk bespoken in the
Moths and butterflies

Did the dripping juice
The grapevine
Gather, galvanize
The guess that grasped
And birthed the asp
That, coiled, watching, lies?

Now writhing, slithers
Hiding: hither
Comes the apex alibi
That biding, tracks
And writing, lacks
No patience; no, he's satisfied

Here lies the skeleton, below
That will not suffer excavation
The last shred of a testament
To epistemic limitation
And never will his pupils capture
Never will the day transpire
With the saints this man was raptured
On the day his grace expired

"I find more bitter than death the woman whose heart is snares and traps, whose hands are chains. Whoever pleases God shall escape from her; but the sinner will be ensnared by her."

(Ecclesiastes 7:26 WEBU)

A crack in the shell

It glimmers, face the image
Take it in and
See the hologram

I grimace, take my vision
Set my limits
And the tryptophan's

An overdose that doses never
To average high and low, "whatever"

Feign indifference, feign desire
Plainly wishing to transpire

And spiraling, perspiring,
Simple! Catastrophize the sting!

And press the barb upon the tail
Upon the tail, to self-assail

The venom's anti-venom
Is the venom, it is the denim

Is the cut, it is the art
Is the face, it is the start

Is the egg, it is the snake
Is the reason I'm awake

"God blessed the seventh day, and made it holy, because he rested in it from all his work of creation which he had done."

(Genesis 2:3 WEBU)

Heatstroke

Gaunt and hollow
Gutted by the heat, and wallowed
Guts gave up the meat I swallowed
Granted, was a treat to follow
Through with scraps of strict intention
Knew I lacked a strong retention
Hewed and hacked away, don't mention
Snooze, on track for long suspension

Academics, devote the day
Economics, give the night
Each demands the greater say
Of creeping,
sleeping,
dead daylight

"The LORD is near to those who have a broken heart,
and saves those who have a crushed spirit."

(Psalms 34:18 WEBU)

Nauseous love

Not sad enough to cry
Not sick enough to throw up
Don't love her enough to know that I love her
But love her too much to give up

"When I was a child, I spoke as a child, I felt as a child, I thought as a child. Now that I have become a man, I have put away childish things."

(1 Corinthians 13:11 WEBU)

20

There was a time when passivity was not a cause for
painful passion.
A time when peace accompanied the primary portion
of a life lived simply.

Sin was foreign,
disagreement unknown,
truth obvious,
and right living circumscribed with care.

Fresh cut grass inches from my nose,
and the heat never disagreeable.

The most natural occupations
were just hard enough
to justify doing them.

...

I cannot profit from the fresh-cut grass.

Peace comes at the price of lost time—
time lost to nebulous potentiality that
screams out in the faces of teenage prodigies.

I am not myself,
but the unfilled mold of a better man I don't have the
will to become.
Sleep is justified with the labor it facilitates,
and security hangs on the maintenance of uninformable
vigilance.

I once saw satisfaction in the foreground,
but I now wear a telescope to bring it back.

My eyesight worsens, and this is the best it will ever
be.
Half of my brain dedicated to the interface
between my eyes and iPhone,
and my iPhone does not have my best interests in
mind.

Who do you remember when golden hours echo
through your headspace?
Does a mother gleam,
a father beam?
Did they remain the giants?

If you are now the giant,
I'm sure you've measured your stature—
its deficit or surplus.
Either leaves an unfavorable taste in one of the two
comparisons—
them to you, you to them.

You may someday be the point of reference—
the giant of more innocent, minuscule eyes.
Will you see through that lie?

Or is the thought—
that the comprehensions of innocence lie to us—
the only lie in play?

The wedding edifice is built on a foundation of petrified
emotion—
of false indifference
held so long
it spoke its own veracity into existence.

Like a cake at the cost of a tongue,
like spectacles at the cost of my spectation,

like the world at the cost of my soul,
I have traded myself for my hope, and will not be
there to receive it.

I wish well upon the man my efforts greet.
May he bathe in the tears of yesteryear.

"But if a man walks in the night, he stumbles, because the light isn't in him."

(John 11:10 WEBU)

And it sets

Clay: "once firm upon the noon"
Ray: "the one who lights the moon"
Day: "I give one gift: my absence"
Blay: "the worm of blissless passion"

Canticle: "in minor key"
Manacled: "to lethargy"
Animal: "annul your right"
Mandible: "give up the fight"

Luca: "borrow energy"
Luna: "swallow empty seas"

Hideous: "you chase a fraction"
Igneous: "embrace inaction"

Star: "recedes the solar sliver"

Tar: "no more the soul delivered"

"In the sweat of thy face shalt thou eat bread, until thou return to the ground: for out of it wast thou taken. For dust thou art; and unto dust shalt thou return."

(Genesis 3:19 Dar)

Blood money

Red runs rampant
My arm is drained
Bank account full
Money blood-stained
Body is aching
Slave to the brain
Love is in ending
Care only for gain

"Death and life are in the power of the tongue;
those who love it will eat its fruit."

(Proverbs 18:21 WEBU)

Resist

Strike and slash and push, resist
Let loose every verbal fist
Don't you hope that you'll be missed?
Anything to grow the list

Where's the pleasure in the hindsight?
Can't comfort what's dead and gone
"Calm down, it will all be alright"
To a man who can't respond

They're here, not waiting in the ending
Not a finish line, or race
Oh, what useless time you're spending
In an afterimage chase

Will your comrades in resentment
Remedy its every source?
Will you recognize pretension
Self-perpetuating force?

Who's the object of the envy
If you disdain what you seek?
For each voiced complaint you lend me
All less justified, more weak

You're not far from what you wanted
But, the gap, however small
Seems the sight of being taunted
From the apathetic all

You're not lost potential, you're not
Too far gone to see your home
It may be a leap, but you've got

All you need to call your own

In the tongue is power
In the vocal folds, your isolation
Folds, gives up its limelight hour
To the first communication

All the best are right here with you
All behind the line of speech
What's it take to face the issue?
As far spreads your voice, your reach

"Why is light given to him who is in misery,
life to the bitter in soul[?]"

(Job 3:20 WEBU)

Suppress

Wrench apart that work of art
And cover the mind that's clear
With books and chores and worldly bores
And really all that's near
Turn the glass obsidian
The panes opaque appear
The sightless soul is now consoled
The peaceful shadows steer
From yes and no opposed, the conflict
Isn't welcome here

"But each one is tempted when he is drawn away by his own lust and enticed. Then the lust, when it has conceived, bears sin. The sin, when it is full grown, produces death."

(James 1:14–15 WEBU)

""Give in""

Kill the statue
Burn the hay
That should keep the
Threat at bay

Drop the image
Dash the clay
See it crash
The ash remains

Of the hearth, that dearth of doing
Of the mold and speckled spores
Their crusted careless spread pursuing
Null and voided "search for more"'s

Trust the figure
Waive the wait
All prudence
Undone create

Overthinking
Stay up late
Let the tense
Unclench, abate

And swipe the card, and slide the cash
And tell indulgence you're a fan
Construct the height from which to crash
The heavy hand of empty plans

"I am forgotten from their hearts like a dead man.
I am like broken pottery."

(Psalms 31:12 WEBU)

Shattered

Broken China doesn't mend
with each shard in position.
Shattered, scattered, now it bends
to live within division,
as not fusion but fission.

"Let not the flood of waters overflow me, neither let the deep swallow me up; and let not the pit shut its mouth upon me."

(Psalms 69:15 Dar)

Surrounded, surrendered

I'm sitting on a beach chair
In the shallows of the ocean
Watching a tsunami
As it starts to close in

And I can run, but I decided
That I like the view
What's prettier than nature's waves
Crashing over you?

And did I mention?—no, I didn't:
There's fire on the land
The flames will quench
But for a moment
When the waves swallow the sand

And then tsunami, flames, and all
Will crash with equal purpose
No longer will my safety stand
It swims weakly through the ocean

Chapter 2
The Other

"The voice of one saying, "Cry out!"
One said, "What shall I cry?"
"All flesh is like grass,
and all its glory is like the flower of the field.
The grass withers,
the flower fades,
because the LORD's breath blows on it.
Surely the people are like grass.
The grass withers,
the flower fades;
but the word of our God stands forever.""

(Isaiah 40:6-8 WEBU)

"Her house is the way to Sheol,
going down to the rooms of death."

(Proverbs 7:27 WEBU)

The flower

You were a flower once.
You were a sprout,
a budding outgrowth of a deeper source.
An apple of the eye of the calmest hour.

If you were chosen,
much laid between the choice
and the voice of your fragrance.
You wore a gown of thorns,
and caution cloaked your course from the grasp of
the interloper.

But you were not content to wear that gown.

What could be smoother than that which waits beneath
the spiny boundary?
What would need such armor
but something wholly soft, one layer below?

And you knew.
You knew the fear they held—
that they would never know the soul beneath the
thorny multitude.
Oh, what a sight you could bring!

What they wouldn't give, they wouldn't be able to
say.
What they would give—
there would be nothing unsaid.
What they would give to know, you would take.

A simple transaction.

With their eager eyes

and your eager coffers
came a gleaming cleaver of choice.
A cleaver chosen.
Two-edged.
There never was a handle.

You were a branch once.
You drank an umbilical vine, and you knew your
petals ripened.
But what more is there for the trampled rose?

Cut off at the waist.
Your spine went to waste,
with the spiny gown you disregarded.
Your colors flowed out of your soul, and back into
your mouth,
like a self-filling siphon—
leaking.

The river runs dry when cycles turn to chains.
Your tree was rooted.
But no matter how much you compose yourself,
you're closed under composition,
and your limit is null.

"For the lips of an adulteress drip honey.
Her mouth is smoother than oil,
but in the end she is as bitter as wormwood,
and as sharp as a two-edged sword."

(Proverbs 5:3-4 WEBU)

The rose

The knife that trimmed the rose's thorn
The rose that grew no longer grows
The blessing when the bud was born
Was cloven, petals decompose

The smoothened stem invites the touch
No crown of thorns adorns the pleasure
The petal profits inasmuch
As it becomes your only treasure

The gaping gap the cut contracted
The spilling veins are paid in cash
The wilting waste, the self-enacted
Value outflow paints the gash

When there were branches bathing, basking
Scattered sunlight saw tomorrow
Extromission everlasting
Cut the vine, on borrowed time
With dripping wine, the gilded crime
But when will you return what's borrowed?

"Who can find a worthy woman?
For her value is far above rubies."

(Proverbs 31:10 WEBU)

enough

Keeper of the
calmest interdiction
Alpha shades the
colors shining through
Maximal
inexorable friction
In between
what isn't and what's due

Fully oriented
to refusal
Unacquainted
with all thus refused
The blackbird's claw
accompanies reproval
The tightened grip imprints,
lightly amused

Figure of the
archetypal other
Unity, community
rebuffed
Interchange,
replace her with another
No repose but knows
she knows no bluff

Yet I wary,
weary of permission
The hand extended
seems a silken cuff
All sufficiently
suggest omission

All I know:
my best is not enough

"For everyone who exalts himself will be humbled, and whoever humbles himself will be exalted."

(Luke 14:11 WEBU)

The fractured idol

Idols of their flesh are built
Of stone
Though stone is known to weather

Hopes in high, exalted sights
Would wilt
Contrite, polite, and measured

Idly, a line is cast
A ray
Mental, intentional, the

Central facet, to imagine
Grasp
Ignite insight, and molded

Behind each fount of admiration
A fear, to face the accusations
A crack, a hairline fracture creeping
The outlook gone, vertigo reaping

"Don't be conformed to this world, but be transformed by
the renewing of your mind, so that you may prove what
is the good, well-pleasing, and perfect will of God."

(Romans 12:2 WEBU)

Acceptance

"Acceptance," a word which positively fails
To convey its positive intent
Because "acceptance" more often entails
Foregoing all things heaven-sent
In favor of things which rack up bails
And lead to the death of those not meant
And even now, I hear their wails—

Acceptance leaves a funny scent

"The sound of a cry from Horonaim,
desolation and great destruction!"

(Jeremiah 48:3 WEBU)

Muted

The production
of destruction
is an effortless construction

Actless actions
make the choice of
ever-absent interaction

Unvoiced vocals,
muddy opals,
glass or gas, both
neon-noble

Serve no service,
nestled,
nervous,
nullify the last deduction

"And again, "The Lord knows the reasoning of the wise, that it is worthless.""

(1 Corinthians 3:20 WEBU)

Rediflection

Alphabetic index
is a shield from honest thought
Dictionary context is appealed to—
now I spot

How reflecting redirects
a truth I should've taken
Not accepting,
all the same I stay, if I don't take in

Simpler than all discursive
methods could expound
Dialectical hallucinations
can confound

Devil on my shoulder
and an angel on my side
And, when I'm the arbiter,
take three on for the ride

I'll imagine that
the whole of discourse has arrived
I'll assume that,
though alone,
I let nothing elide

Encyclopedia inscriptions
crowd the clear of glasses
If the air is noxious,
words compose the opaque gasses

Heights of the elite can climb to
submersible depths

Towers of a silken tusk are
towers carved of death

Pulp and printing pile up
enough to block the sun
It's hard to care for seeing
when you've got a world to run

70

"Whatever your hand finds to do, do it with your might; for there is no work, nor plan, nor knowledge, nor wisdom, in Sheol, where you are going."

(Ecclesiastes 9:10 WEBU)

To Reconcile

Reconciliation was
Two lights, two bright white
Beams at dusk

But my realization was
Not slight, not quite right
Beige and rust

That sat still where my hopes had lain
That took the place of pallid paint
And dashed with feather-pillow-shouts
The hope of clearing up the doubt

That car is not the seat of glory
Not a throne at which to plead
That car is not the one that knows me
Now the void can plant the seed

And unsaid sayings stay unsaid
The grave concerns? Graves hold the dead
The poison placement plainly pled
That my perspective laced with lead

Should stay intoxicated with
The worst of all caught in the sieve

"LORD, I know that the way of man is not in himself.
It is not in man who walks to direct his steps."

(Jeremiah 10:23 WEBU)

Poppies

Poppies sprouted in her steps;
I choked upon the pollen
They gently gestured to the glade
Where not a leaf had fallen

Amidst the auburn forest fluttered
Passive honeybees
They made their nest in branches green
Among the apple trees

Their fruit was bitter on my tongue
I sought to taste instead
The honey, as the offspring of
The newfound flower bed

The hive parted the apple trees
That part the barren brush
I plucked and chewed the comb while droned
The bees' unbroken hush

The bite was viscous in my mouth
I tasted legs and wings
The honey heavy on my lips
Now peppered red with stings

Concentric ringed vegetation
Crowned the one shock left
The forest queen returned the look
And shook the shibboleth

I pulled my face up from the poppies
Stood, and saw no hint
Of anything resembling

The forest queen's footprint

"Two are better than one, because they have a good reward for their labor. For if they fall, the one will lift up his fellow; but woe to him who is alone when he falls, and doesn't have another to lift him up. Again, if two lie together, then they have warmth; but how can one keep warm alone? If a man prevails against one who is alone, two shall withstand him; and a threefold cord is not quickly broken."

(Ecclesiastes 4:9–12 WEBU)

78

Third Places

Together
Know I'd better
No, I've never
I've not seen the sight

Gateless
Grass and pavement
And the faceless
Morning, evening, night

Needless of justification
Stretched out on the living plains
Emptied of their occupations
Strangers to the empty pains

Simple
Not a symbol
Trace the dimples
In their smiling faces

Nexus
Of connections
The collective
In collective spaces

When the hour shuns the sunbeam
When it gives the moon its leave
Still, the corpus runs, the one stream
Of all vigor you'd conceive

El propósito: hablar
El objeto de la lucha
La ausencia de lucha

Mi gente como el mar

Chapter 3

To Thwart Damnation

"He said to them, "I saw Satan having fallen like lightning from heaven…""

(Luke 10:18 WEBU)

"For our wrestling is not against flesh and blood, but against the principalities, against the powers, against the world's rulers of the darkness of this age, and against the spiritual forces of wickedness in the heavenly places."

(Ephesians 6:12 WEBU)

THE HUNTER

Heavy footfall followed he
Who called himself the hunter.
In dimming darkness made his march
Upon the clap of thunder.
The grasses shriveled in the fields
Where lambs and oxen graze.
The sun had fled in maddened fear;
The moon in blackened phase.

But heavier than trespass or
The hunter's stolid stance,
And just beyond periphery:
There flowed a petric glance.
The hunter traveled, ignorant,
Beyond the octagon;
An inmate of the fallen star,
The pale panopticon.

Raring was the reaper to
Protect his carnal pride.
In hubris held he confidence
He had not justified.
The common enemy of man
At this, provoked a nod:
"The lightning scars that light your path
Are fit to be your god."

Blazing was the shadow
Underneath the hallowed wing.
Scorching was the sunlight
That rebuked the suffering.
Molten was the javelin;
To vapor went his glare.

Fallen was the hunter
Of the power of the air.

"Then Jesus said to him, "Put your sword back into its place, for all those who take the sword will die by the sword."

(Matthew 26:52 WEBU)

RECKLESS

Do you ever find yourself
RECKLESS?

Scraping point to path beneath
Cherish heft that left the sheath
RECKLESS

Downturned eyes, and aim downcast
In advance: the omniclast
RECKLESS

Severed soul despised tomorrow
Agent of the serpent's sorrow
RECKLESS

War in heaven waged in thought—
Impotent oneironaut.

"A simple man believes everything,
but the prudent man carefully considers his ways."

(Proverbs 14:15 WEBU)

"For the time will come when they will not listen to the
sound doctrine, but having itching ears, will heap up for
themselves teachers after their own lusts..."
(2 Timothy 4:3 WEBU)

Arcana

Spores that sprout and spread their trespass
Colonize and replicate
Mold will show how long the dead last
Disinfectants obfuscate

Snowmelt frees a long-held captive
Captive now to captive eyes
Captive cell, the host is trapped in
Captivate: attractive lies

Wisdom knows what makes attractions
Folly takes the word of one
Wisdom sees the undone actions
Folly sees itself undone

Folly fears consideration
Folly treats as false what's real
Wisdom knows but one vexation:
Folly's hands are at the wheel

Rob the tomb and taste the plunder
Feed the scourge in every tooth
No, the rot is not a wonder
Not all secrets tell the truth

"Yet you don't know what your life will be like tomorrow.
For what is your life? For you are a vapor that appears for
a little time and then vanishes away."

(James 4:14 WEBU)

cliffside

A pebble tumbles down the cliff,
dislodging gravel as it travels,
And a man now questions whether
rocks could presage any message.
As it passes further, wins the
mounting din of troubled kin and
I cannot distinguish
that one rebel from the rest.

Seven thousand
thousand thousand
thousand thousand
thousand grains—
nothing but circumferential dust.
Hades' ocean calmly bears
the unseen pillars of the deep
to keep *imago dei* upon the crust.

But if I fall and pierce the mantle—
plunge the bone in molten stone—
I would differ little from
the slightest fervor in the foam.

"The light shines in the darkness, and the darkness hasn't overcome it."

(John 1:5 WEBU)

Pity the soul

Pity the soul that jumps the cliff
and drowns itself in darkness
Glittering golden petroglyphs
may crown the vaulted ports
Heavy, the hold; how manic
man may sound when he regards this
Heavy as pitch; emboldened,
listen, hear the loud retorts

Where goes the goading cry,
whereby you sought the dark's advance?
Know you alone will die,
reflect all that you necromance
In mires wallow,
flightless swallow,
muddied feathers
caked in leather
Would that you would shake the fetters,
would that you would take the letters

Would that you would fly again
Leave the dark behind, my friend

""Therefore behold, the days come", says the LORD, "that it will no more be called 'Topheth' or 'The valley of the son of Hinnom', but 'The valley of Slaughter'; for they will bury in Topheth until there is no place to bury.""

(Jeremiah 7:32 WEBU)

Hinnom

Asherah,
Your altar stained in conscious concupiscence

Baal,
You fail to deaden tears; I hear our burning infants

Moloch,
May your blood pool cold; your eyes drain dry; your
strength supine

Aphrodite,
Birthed and killed the children of the mighty

No, in your hallowed, sacred bed
In Hinnom, where their skulls were spread
I will recall the clouds that cleared
You will appall, and stand in fear

And give account, in judgment then:
No ally in the lion's den

"For God so loved the world, that he gave his only born Son, that whoever believes in him should not perish, but have eternal life. For God didn't send his Son into the world to judge the world, but that the world should be saved through him. He who believes in him is not judged. He who doesn't believe has been judged already, because he has not believed in the name of the only born Son of God. This is the judgment, that the light has come into the world, and men loved the darkness rather than the light, for their works were evil."

(John 3:16-19 WEBU)

"for he is our God.
We are the people of his pasture,
and the sheep in his care.
Today, oh that you would hear his voice!
Don't harden your heart, as at Meribah,
as in the day of Massah in the wilderness,"

(Psalms 95:7-8 WEBU)

hell

The sands of time
The sediment
The mile-high rock wall

The pantomime
Of precedent
Of change, no change at all

A bird will pass
Each century
He leaves with sharpened jaw

The hourglass
He meant to me
I hear the buzzard's caw

How long it takes
A dialect
To draw out from a drawl

What change you'd make
Might you expect
To fly beyond a crawl?

To tally, take in
Every tick
Beyond a humble scrawl

Don't trust your patience
Don't predict
It drones, don't heed its call

No paragon of perseverance
I'm the scarecrow's flesh

I was the sole soul standing
When the holy half was threshed

Don't take it at the first appearance
You're in luck it's fresh
And from the fall, the landing
Onto every fallen crest

He gave his life on bended knee
And all it took was "yes"
And I forewent that single word
I traded life for death

I forfeited eternity
Destiny manifest
No dialogue, you won't be heard
Give up the search for rest

So here's Gehenna, settle in
You won't get used to it
The valley of the shadow
The waste, the burning pit

Here's Hades, concentrate the sin
The flame was always lit
Fondly recall the gallows
Picture the word "exit"

Here's Sheol, isn't she a beauty?
She'll show the opposite
You can't stay past your welcome, and
You'll know all consequence

Abandon pleasure's memory
You can't chase after it
You're bound by only one command

You'll need none more than grit

So grit your teeth
You'll never lose them
Though they fall, they'll find persistence

Underneath
The land of loose ends
You will stay, despite resistance

Let it loose
Fill your lungs freely
Whether you cough, or suffocate

To tell the truth
You'll never need me
To endlessly pontificate

Because the endless ends right here
And know that when I say it "ends"
I mean that I will cease describing
What sight could show, what ears could hear

And I cannot make myself clear
And no, the truth I will not bend
Ensure against the soon arriving
Now is the time, now is the year

"because that which is known of God is revealed in them, for God revealed it to them. For the invisible things of him since the creation of the world are clearly seen, being perceived through the things that are made, even his everlasting power and divinity, that they may be without excuse. Because knowing God, they didn't glorify him as God, and didn't give thanks, but became vain in their reasoning, and their senseless heart was darkened."

(Romans 1:19-21 WEBU)

Gateway Oceanic

Pearlescent
in the amniotic ocean
Abyssally abysmal,
undeclared
An unexamined present premise
capped the benthic plains
And midnight
left the sailors unaware

The sonar swept the sky
and not the waters
And in that space
devoid of angels' light
The telescope aimed at the sun
grew unbearably hotter
Psychosomatic shivers
born of spite

The geothermal slit that splits
the miry mid-Atlantic
Unguarded,
glows where disenchantment dies
And kills the chill
that frosts the thoughts
that seek to speak romantic
More pungent
as the boiled vapors rise

If, in the fabric, seams can stretch,
allow the offered rift
Don't mend the blessed
tearing of the curtain
And if the territory suffers

continental drift
Don't fear corrosion of
what once was certain

The tides grow choppy,
brave the spray
invoked with plate tectonics
The magma melts its
mark upon the sands
The sonar and the telescope
not blinded by the rains
Now face
what they begin to understand

104

"For the Son of Man came to seek and to save that which was lost."

(Luke 19:10 WEBU)

DESCENT

Far out, past the
patterned street lamps sleeping
Leagues beyond the
nearest gaze of man
In the winds where
silence turns to weeping
All waste,
where none can trace the unmarked span

Attentive to
the null and deadened speaker
Rust receives the
refuse of the bog
I became the
landscape and the creature
With the roots all
rotten in the fog

To the anechoic
enervation
Into the void you
brought the dawn's descent
The corners whispered
passive desecration
That withered more
the farther down you went

In the desperate depths,
decomposition
Delineates
inversion's darkened turf
But every person
pleading your petition

Received the substitution
of your worth

Buried
as the seed before the sprouting
But
the shell did not mean you were bound
Desperate depths
did not bring desperate shouting
No,
you came to stare the darkness down

"Where, O death, [is] thy sting? where, O death, thy victory?"

(1 Corinthians 15:55 Dar)

Easter

On that day
When truth was slain
The sky, as one, forgot the day
No longer could the veil sustain
The rocks could not but crumble

The dead did raise
Living displays
Without the son,
all stunned remain
The only one,
lifeless did lay
Yet not once did He stumble

With time, He'll rot
Or so they thought
No light, no sight,
yet those were not
A hindrance to the one beyond
Now Satan asks for mercy

For his clothing,
cast their lots
'Round the tomb
guards took their spots
The sun rose
to an absent God
That solemn sun still burning

Their doors were locked,
their gates were barred
Their hopes,
like his two hands,

were scarred
They quivered,
sunlight shivered,
stars
Alone were left,
the blue was charred
El día sin mi Dios

But though
the son of God was marred
And even He,
not free from harm
The wrath had passed, and,
clothed in nard
Out from the grave did He go

And ate with them,
the fish and bread
From death to living,
so doing, fed
That we,
now free,
no longer dead
Could live like death forgot us

A human
but no less Godhead
With nothing
that He hadn't said
God spoke,
He woke,
no longer bled
Was stained to make us spotless

112

"How you have fallen from heaven, shining one, son of the dawn! How you are cut down to the ground, who laid the nations low! You said in your heart, "I will ascend into heaven! I will exalt my throne above the stars of God! I will sit on the mountain of assembly, in the far north! I will ascend above the heights of the clouds! I will make myself like the Most High!" Yet you shall be brought down to Sheol, to the depths of the pit."

(Isaiah 14:12-15 WEBU)

MESSIAH

"I will rise above the heavens
Exalt the mirrored throne
I will be the six in seven
A third will be my own
I will make a new confession
Silence the shouting stones
I will trade for truth, deception
In men's hearts make my home"
Listen, wisdom, learn the lesson
In wilderness he roamed
But I saw Satan fall from Heaven
To outer darkness thrown

The living water on the land
Has crushed the serpent's head
On sea He stands, on angels' hands
On scorpions He treads
And through the belly of the sand
"Behold, the sky is red"
The words of trust of man in man
Death could not cut the thread

Behold, now, making all things new
I looked,
and no more sea
As if the waters parted through
Were soaked up by the tree
The tree of life begins anew
And evermore will be
The bride is pure before the groom
The final unity

"I saw a mighty angel proclaiming with a loud voice, "Who is worthy to open the book, and to break its seals?" No one in heaven above, or on the earth, or under the earth, was able to open the book or to look in it. Then I wept much, because no one was found worthy to open the book or to look in it. One of the elders said to me, "Don't weep. Behold, the Lion who is of the tribe of Judah, the Root of David, has overcome: he who opens the book and its seven seals."

I saw in the middle of the throne and of the four living creatures, and in the middle of the elders, a Lamb standing, as though it had been slain, having seven horns and seven eyes, which are the seven Spirits of God, sent out into all the earth."

(Revelation 5:2-6 WEBU)

WHO?

Who will bring the beast to shore?
Who will roll away the stone?
Who will tear the seven seals?
Who is worthy to atone?

Who rebukes the torrent's roar?
Who can tame the winds with breath?
Who can make the heavens kneel?
Who could not be held by death?

Who speaks to the permutations?
Who sets them on a single path?
Who looks down on Cantor's crown?
Who kindles purpose in their wrath?

Who foresaw the perturbations?
Who can act through opposition?
He took the form of dust and ground
And tore the curtain of partition

"Therefore the Father loves me, because I lay down my life, that I may take it again. No one takes it away from me, but I lay it down by myself. I have power to lay it down, and I have power to take it again. I received this commandment from my Father."

(John 10:17-18 WEBU)

His Own Accord

The curtain torn,
the untorn cloak
His breath failed
when His body broke.

Twelve thousand angels
stilled the sword
Unflinching
as men killed the Lord.

The triumph
when the failure spoke:
The form,
disfigured,
fresh,
awoke.

With every southward step you roamed
A voice cried out behind—
"come home."

"Behold, he is coming with the clouds, and every eye will see him, including those who pierced him. All the tribes of the earth will mourn over him. Even so, Amen."

(Revelation 1:7 WEBU)

Dissolve

I was crouching at the door.
Dripping, panting, pooling, puddled,
Muddled, shocked in muddy socks,
I reveled in the equinox.

But I was crushed upon the rock.
I was hung upon the tree.
Number me with those who mock,
Yet I renounce my revelry.

And how could I remember me?
A cloud descends above:
The noon was dark; my reveries
Were drowned in fearsome love.

Against the coming infinite,
I know not who I am.
Hear He who melts the mountains:
Face the army of the Lamb.

"In this is love, not that we loved God, but that he loved us, and sent his Son as the atoning sacrifice for our sins."

(1 John 4:10 WEBU)

122

A Debt

Transactive transgression
Left with the impression
Our credit cards never run out

Beauty notwithstanding
Demeanor demanding
The wolf of our flesh has grown stout

When solid ground's gone
And grim sounds the gong
And of all our bearings without

A debt was incurred by the sum of our wrongs
And none of it left with the Son on the cross
Emptied all we worried about
In a moment surpassed the devout

"But as it is written,
"Things which an eye didn't see, and an ear didn't hear,
which didn't enter into the heart of man,
these God has prepared for those who love him.""

(1 Corinthians 2:9 WEBU)

The Choice

The concrete piers
Unchosen peers
And yesterday was now

The selfsame years
And distant jeers
And you'd forgotten how

There was a day
A time, a place
When you'd tomorrow seek

But then you stayed
The price you paid
The seconds turned to weeks

The weeks were months
And years they made
The years were just
A tenth-decade
The decades seemed to creep and pounce
And seek a total that amounts
To eighty, yes, they'd take it all
Take everything, but—
check the wall?

Glowing parallelogram?
Birds and luminescent sand?
A silence louder than the shouts?
A keyless
doorless
all-way-out?

Why don't they see it?
Am I alone?
And how did nothing carve the stone?
Why the peace,
and why for me?
Without a lock,
without a key?

And through the threshold
I'm beyond it
Through the glass
and past the comet
Earth's a piece of truth,
or was
I was never just stardust

I don't need reduced exposure
Prison didn't ask for closure
Left the home of every fighter
Nothing hurts,
it's growing brighter

Warmth will never be too hot
The air cool to the touch,
and I'm not
Asking for more eyes behind me
Left it,
bright and never blinding

Time is slow
if real at all
Feel the feeling
of it all
—Paradise with no withdrawal

"Where could I go from your Spirit?
Or where could I flee from your presence?"

(Psalms 139:7 WEBU)

Inhabited

Where gasses with metallic lusters
Dot the solemn superclusters

From crushing depths of magma chambers
To bare calderas, cracked and cratered

Where molten rain precipitates
On freezing wakes of methane lakes

With sulfur shores of breathless vapor
There, the matter meets the maker

Chapter 4

Partake

130

"How beautiful on the mountains are the feet of him
who brings good news,
who publishes peace,
who brings good news,
who proclaims salvation,
who says to Zion, "Your God reigns!""

(Isaiah 52:7 WEBU)

Dust

The dust kicks up
in shapeless billows;
(Shades of copper,
tan, and gray)
Suspension of the
sand and clay
That settles on the dusty pillows

Gravel crunches,
seems to pray;
With deference to
the heavy shoes
Of those who sprinted,
spreading news
From clouds of stone to ocean spray

Dust we are, and
to the dust
It is our duty
to return
The toils summed
do duly earn
No more or less than toils must

Perhaps,
as ashes in the urn,
To someday float
as formless dirt
To be,
and hold no high alert
I'll scatter as the trampled fern

But down at the

disciples' feet
Where sandals and the
soil meet
Arises,
where apostles were,
The ground that bears the messenger

"for a righteous man falls seven times and rises up again,
but the wicked are overthrown by calamity."

(Proverbs 24:16 WEBU)

To Return

It is not that you fell
No, your feet found their place
Though you saw your grip loosen
Know loose isn't releasing
And the sevenfold fall
Is the righteous one's race
Though pausing, you must
Ensure stopping's not ceasing

"Iron sharpens iron;
so a man sharpens his friend's countenance."

(Proverbs 27:17 WEBU)

Sanctifire

Furnace flows now indiffuse,
Skim the dross and sift the sluice;
I was ore, and lacked a luster
Fire bore the sprouting mustard.

Fruitless as though neophytic,
Born to breach the paralytic
Stagnancy; I would not settle.
Wear the strength of tempered metal.

Scourge and thin the spreading reach;
Shear—no, execute the leech.
Steel has sharpened steel to gold;
Now the branch may bear the cold.

He sears the weakness of the flesh
And casts as far as east from west
To kill the dread that seeks infection
And wills the dead to resurrection.

"Go to the ant, you sluggard.
Consider her ways, and be wise;
which having no chief, overseer, or ruler,
provides her bread in the summer,
and gathers her food in the harvest."

(Proverbs 6:6-8 WEBU)

The Slow Burn

I am grateful for the tire
That rocks across my weary soul
School, then work, then quench the fire
When my focus takes its toll
When I'm driven, I'm inspired
It's the slow burn I extol

"Your eyes saw my body.
In your book they were all written,
the days that were ordained for me,
when as yet there were none of them."

(Psalms 139:16 WEBU)

Will I?

Jigsaw saw bands sing their song
And mildly malignant
They cut their carvings from the log
And printers paste the pigment

And now, greeted with the outlines
Pick and stumble, place, repair
Steps are guesses, traced without lines
All will unified declare:

Traced to taste a sweeter wine
That ages with the effort passing
Painting from the precut pine
As long as your patience lasting

With the thought nervously held
Hope my effort is my will
Hope that my ideals should meld
With all my "I'll die on that hill"

"For every creature of God is good, and nothing is to be rejected if it is received with thanksgiving."

(1 Timothy 4:4 WEBU)

The Antisceticist

I asked the heart that skipped a beat,
"Who architects elation?
Who in the dark invoked the heat and
wove the first sensation?"

It answered, "I am but a mind
that wades in heady fragrance.
I sought a higher way, a kind
of brighter, whiter pavement.
I do as well as you'd surmise
to analyze the nascent,
and cull, lest from me should arise
a knife in pleasant valence."

I told it, "Chiaroscuritic
portraiture may stir your soul,
but when you name the constant critic
as "corazón," your constant role
may cast aside the truer fount
from whom aesthetics came to be!
You call corrupt what may amount
to treating God contemptibly!"

It frowned, and then it looked around,
and saw the good it had dismissed.
It blushed, and then, its patience rushed,
embraced the nearest foggy mist.

I laughed, and said, "You've much to learn,
but take my hand, you have a say.
You're not a mind, but you are mine;
you bring the color to my gray.
Your enterprise: the gentle cries

console you best when weary.
Forget not He whose sole concern:
that you see Him more clearly."

Chapter 5

Loss

"For you formed my inmost being.
You knit me together in my mother's womb.
I will give thanks to you,
for I am fearfully and wonderfully made.
Your works are wonderful.
My soul knows that very well.
My frame wasn't hidden from you,
when I was made in secret,
woven together in the depths of the earth."

(Psalms 139:13–15 WEBU)

Six months only

Life's first cry and final sigh—
They weren't that far apart.
Six months came; the beating tamed
To stop what six weeks starts.
And if the frame should lack your name—
Your lungs no life impart,
And fluttered eyes to shuttered skies
Close up your quickened heart,

I'll count my hours, count my blessings,
Clasp my brothers close;
Draw out meaning from your screaming
Heaven holds your ghost;
Loosely leaning on the beaming
Head that once was host
To helpless power, growth regressing;
Break Abaddon's boast.

"He has put my brothers far from me.
My acquaintances are wholly estranged from me.
My relatives have gone away.
My familiar friends have forgotten me."

(Job 19:13-14 WEBU)

Owen

Dear absent,
It happens to happen to be
That you are not someone who's happened to me

And forthcoming,
Your face a veritable fiction
I can't conjure a human with elegant diction

But present
I see what I never saw yet
Not foreshadowed,
let's say we saw and we met

And let's make up the time
And the times not yet through
And the times we both will enter into

And when you cry
know I'm beside you
To kick my face
so as to guide you
From the tearful
into laughter
I'm the fence to greener pastures

Your hardest punch
will make me chuckle
Your tiny fist,
your squishy knuckle
And I'll pretend that I've been bested—
That my heartbeat has been arrested

I'll seem a giant;

You'll seem as you are
And the giants of giants bring cookies and cards
The turf is a carpet,
we'll run through the yard
And I know one of us will find a glass shard
And with tweezers,
the clean-up won't be that hard
It'll all cauterize
when barefoot on the tar

You'll be asking—I'll answer
You'll be learning—I'll know
You'll be playing—I'll earn
You'll be growing—I'm grown
You'll be sleeping—I'll rock you
You'll be frightened—Big hug
You'll be hungry—I'll feed you
You'll be crying—Ears plugged

You'll be you and you won't be
and you will not remember
You'll be growing without me
and you'll cool off the embers
And the fire you came from
will cease to exist
And that tiny knuckle
on that minuscule fist
Will open to let out a spark,
jumps intently
And the leaves,
all the kindling,
warmly and gently
Cook to a crisp
as they faithfully glow
The charcoal I am,

though I'm not,
is your own

"Love is patient and is kind.   Love doesn't envy. Love doesn't brag, is not proud, doesn't behave itself inappropriately, doesn't seek its own way, is not provoked, takes no account of evil; doesn't rejoice in unrighteousness, but rejoices with the truth; bears all things, believes all things, hopes all things, and endures all things."

(1 Corinthians 13:4–7 WEBU)

stillborn

All at once
our lives are lived
What was,
still is,
is here
All my trust,
it lies within
That sweet,
uneasy cheer

I press play,
I'm hearing when
She sought
that I should hear
I vibrate through uncertainty
A gentle hope is reared

The stillborn son
of two in one
I see him breathe sometimes
I hold him close, say
"It's not done
I won't leave you to die"

And CPR is what I'm giving
Trample the thought of my misgivings
Confusing grief is what I'm living
Joy at the sight of my relivings

And hope is here
And hope's not dead
The stillborn son
With a gentle head

"The cords of death surrounded me.
The floods of ungodliness made me afraid."

(Psalms 18:4 WEBU)

A Voice

I heard a voice upon the breeze
And squinted,
then I knew who called.
They reached across the canopies
And rang out through enclosing walls.

The single thought within the noise
The only order in the waves
I sought to know what was employed
To give back what they freely gave.

But couldn't make a recompense
And as the echoes died away
I shouted
"I did not intend
To forfeit all unto the fray!"

And from the breeze
came no reply.
I hung my head;
the wind had died.
I knew that I
could not rely
On what had not
on me relied.

"Behold, if he slay me, yet would I trust in him; but I will defend mine own ways before him."

(Job 13:15 Dar)

Still, My God is Good

Calamity is unaddressed
And still, my God is good
It's not a trial, not a test
Yet still, my God is good

Meaninglessness can attest
The purpose I can only guess
To all of it I will confess
That still, my God is good

What the worst will bring to mind:
Thank God my God is good
Not a step before I find
I know my God is good

In the least it all aligns
The wicked twist they call a line
The straight, upright, today reminds
Me that my God is good

Understand, absent a plan
The will of God is good
My highest hopes are not in man
But in a God who's good

From the fallout one still stands
The eyes imply no reprimand
And in my reach an outstretched hand
—I see my God is good

Chapter 6

The Tranquil

"Set your mind on the things that are above, not on the things that are on the earth."

(Colossians 3:2 WEBU)

Serenity

Close your eyes and see
What open eyes obscured
Now note with clarity
What mounted frames had blurred

All given uninterpreted
All taken,
I observed
As clothed purposive,
stirred to sin
And passively disturbed

I closed my eyes
and in broad daylight
Claimed serenity I'd lost
With determined inner eyesight
Cast my burden to the cross

"The life of the body is a heart at peace,
but envy rots the bones."

(Proverbs 14:30 WEBU)

The Only Silent Silence

Hear the sound of nothing,
Sound of every stray reflection

Feel the urges absent
And no rush for self-inspection

Shadows only calming
Telling me to rest my head

Streetlights warmly watching
Neither to nor from they led

No one calls or needs me
Neither do I need myself

Nothing left compelling
And unto nothing compelled

Finally, it's silent
Silent as it always was

When I, too deaf to hear it
With ever-aural mistrust

Could not help but
Treat the voices

Of each each and all my
Unmade choices

Could not help but
Wonder always

That's a world of

Echo-hallways

Echo-hallways
Half-locked doors

Tile ceilings
Tile floors

I've a mind of
Knitted blankets

Thought and care
For thoughtless statements

Where all the warmth
Is all my own

But sleeping,
All my fears are shown

That they're the dreams
And I'm the dreamer

And sleeping, I'm a
Daylight-seeker

I awake to woolen peace
Apprehensions only dreams

"In peace I will both lay myself down and sleep,
for you alone, LORD, make me live in safety."

(Psalms 4:8 WEBU)

Sueño

Put on the face of peace and sleep
Let sorrows fade and torments weep
For none can reach your sleeping cares
You lay beneath a kinder air

"They also who dwell in faraway places are afraid at your wonders. You call the morning's dawn and the evening with songs of joy."

(Psalms 65:8 WEBU)

Comforter

Now sleeps the sun
Till in morning it wakes
Sleep soundly and trust
You in little hold stakes
Goodnight to the stars
Or how few you see
And the rush of the cars
Let all fade, and sleep

"Above all these things, walk in love, which is the bond of perfection."

(Colossians 3:14 WEBU)

Monothoughtful

Absent intention, without willing, I find
You are the constant tenant of my mind

Chapter 7

Within and Without

"Behold, I stand at the door and knock. If anyone hears my voice and opens the door, then I will come in to him and will dine with him, and he with me."

(Revelation 3:20 WEBU)

HouseHold

The house isn't what it used to be.

Sidestep shingles peppering the cracked concrete,
shards shape the well-worn walkway.

Far exceeding the walk as the crow flies,
unrestricted by the optimal camino,
waves away from the door as if trying
and failing
to redirect the pedestrian
far,
far away.

Unsuccessful.

Thank goodness for the bolt.
That door wouldn't stay closed without it.
A chain,
a flap,
a clasp,
three levels of deterrence to keep out all that wants
in.
Why would it want in?

Indistinguishable from the climate of the outdoors;
a microcosm of industrial concentration with none
of its benefits;
stripped of its natural connotations
and unrestored to any others.

The air is conditioned to the tune of ten million fungal
lineages,
seasoned with a concentrated blast of filterable HEPA
targets.

Wise to its target,
well-versed in the ways of its enemy,
and aiming the gun at itself.

Is it shelter
if the door exits to freedom?
Protection from what elements?
The
elementally atomic constitutionally indivisible subdivisionally
exact specifications
at the base of it all seek decay!

"[F]or God is not a God of confusion but of peace, as in all the assemblies of the saints."

(1 Corinthians 14:33 WEBU)

Withinsanity

Flits of dreams,
profanities
The headspace of
insanities
The paraconscious
paranoia
Paradoxes planned to be

The norms of all futures mundane
Astounding,
is it not insane?
It's not;
it's always been this way
It all without me would retain

The frame,
the fiber,
filigree
The fast-fixated poetry
Not daunted,
nothing daunts the airbrush
Tunnels of the willow be

At home,
though every home they damage
Curse on every sapling planted
Taking root,
the yard is barren
All sights of the plant recanted

Peace,
where illogic is logic
Peace,

reflections find their home
Peace,
the filters filter freely
Peace sensation in my bones

184

"The heart is deceitful above all things
and it is exceedingly corrupt.
Who can know it?"

(Jeremiah 17:9 WEBU)

"I"

I feel the mist,
it's sharp
The wind,
it starts
The mist and wind collude
I'm left with barren skin
Of heat,
I lack
And I'm on track to lose
The privilege of an inward eye
The privilege of an inward "I"
Can't say it's cold in summer sunshine
Or that it burns in polar nighttime

Igloos melt to keep me warm
But igloo melts are only formed
When molded from the ground beneath
When "outer" gives "inner" relief
And igloo campfires owe their debt
To solar mandates,
they're beset
With deference nonnegotiable
They can't pretend,
they must behold

How the grasses pay their rent
How a privileged place maintains
If,
within,
the pure is spent
Is not the outside ever-stained?

"Who am I?"

you ask, inquire
Yet who are you if not within
A context?
Is it not required,
A universe for living in?

To see yourself,
you find the mirror
And always faithful,
always clearer
Than the image you had pictured
Than the "you" you took as scripture
Yet,
the mirror sits outside
Yourself,
you are two things, beside
Each other only do both function
Only finished at the junction

"But if anyone thinks that he knows anything, he doesn't yet know as he ought to know."

(1 Corinthians 8:2 WEBU)

Emergent, Shattered

Pyramids and ziggurats and
Eiffel and the Empire State
Structured structures all visibly
Some sense of order relate

And infrastructures, architecture
Set in metal, set in stone
Hold no place in conversation
Though occupants may set the tone

Earth quakes,
and a window's shattered
Well,
much more in an earthquake
And none retain a mundane conference
Chaos—
they do tend to make

Slideshows no longer the focus
When all to the wind was thrown
Memo absence—
foregone presence
Not yet clear what they've been shown

There was no true fallen office
It was symbols on the page
There were no now workless workers
I was a semantic mage

But, for a moment,
you imagined
It was clear,
the thoughts your own

The abstract in your modal workspace
Realized from unknown unknowns

How easy it is to tear down
Suspension of disbelief
Lives of fictional endeavors
Ending as we undeceive

How easily the abstract falters
And,
to face the chaos then
Reaches past what you were built for
—Taunts the limit of the pen

"For you have made him a little lower than the angels,
and crowned him with glory and honor.
You make him ruler over the works of your hands.
You have put all things under his feet…"

(Psalms 8:5-6 WEBU)

Pinnacle

From reaction to intention
Found our bearings, not to mention
Found our honor from our will
Found our freedom in our skill

Insight is our sole invention
Gifted us with comprehension
Left the rest, all forced to kill
We aren't bound to breathe with gills

All our aims are split, dividing
Together with our wit, providing
We don't need their imitations
Expand the scope of our creations

"For to him who is joined with all the living there is hope; for a living dog is better than a dead lion."

(Ecclesiastes 9:4 WEBU)

Pessoptimism

Microscope is macroscoping
Histrionic history of
Individuals are coping
They think insignificantly

Ratio of constant progress
Never climbs the hierarchy
Of ever-faster-growing-process
—Stable place is functioning

To keep us where we did begin
And end before the sun has set
On norms and futures we lived in
While *espera* retains the "yet"

The countables are *tan pesado*
The countable infinities
Will grow a shell that leaves them hollow
Bound down by their worth beneath

If every glory shines its crisis
At forever's waking breaths
And counting up, it wanes, the brightness
Scarcifies what all is left

Then I'll reflect while disembodied
On the shouts in atmospheres
That found their home without the rocky
Three steps from the smoke that cleared

And spread their reach but
Lost their sources
Lost cohesion

Lost their voices

Sunny days are golden years
Even though the megayears
To gigayears and terayears
May give way to petayears

The Petri dish is in a cupboard
The Petri dish will not survive
The Petri dish potential smothered—
The Petri dish is still alive

Bibliography

The Mirror
Psalms 8:4–6; 115:4–8

Sisyphus
Genesis 2:18
James 1:2–4

Ravine
Psalms 28:1; 30:3, 9; 40:2; 69:15; 88:4–6
Jeremiah 2:13; 17:13
John 4:10; 14:6

They still stand
Genesis 3:14
Psalms 22:6

can't
Genesis 2:18
Psalms 147:17

The Basilisk
Genesis 3:1, 5–7
1 Peter 5:8

A crack in the shell
Ecclesiastes 7:26

Heatstroke
Genesis 2:3
Exodus 20:8–11
Leviticus 23:3
Deuteronomy 5:12–14

Luke 23:56

Nauseous love
Psalms 34:18; 73:26; 147:3
Proverbs 17:22
Philippians 4:6-7
1 Peter 5:7
Revelation 21:4

20
Job 16:16
Psalms 6:6; 30:5
Ecclesiastes 3:4
Matthew 16:26; 19:4-6
Romans 5:3-4
1 Corinthians 13:11

And it sets
Psalms 30:5; 88:12
Isaiah 8:22
Lamentations 3:2
John 11:10; 12:35

Blood money
Genesis 3:17-19
Psalms 127:2
Matthew 6:19, 24
Luke 16:13
1 Timothy 6:10

Resist
Psalms 133:1
Proverbs 15:4; 16:24; 18:21
Ecclesiastes 4:9-12
Galatians 5:22

enough
Genesis 2:18, 22–24
Deuteronomy 24:5
Proverbs 31:10
Mark 10:6–9
1 Corinthians 7:2; 11:11

The fractured idol
Exodus 20:4
1 Samuel 16:7
Psalms 115:4–8
Proverbs 16:18; 18:12
Isaiah 2:12; 14:14–15
Jeremiah 49:16
Luke 14:11
1 Corinthians 10:12
Revelation 3:17

Acceptance
Romans 12:2

Muted
Jeremiah 48:3
Hebrews 10:25

Rediflection
Proverbs 14:23; 28:26
Ecclesiastes 1:18; 6:8; 10:1
1 Corinthians 3:20

To Reconcile
Ecclesiastes 9:10
Matthew 5:23–24

Poppies

Genesis 3:6–7
Judges 12:6
Proverbs 5:3; 31:3
Jeremiah 10:23

Third Places
Ecclesiastes 4:9–12
Hebrews 10:25

THE HUNTER
Genesis 4:23–24; 10:8–9
Joshua 8:26
1 Samuel 17:45
1 Chronicles 1:10
Job 39:23; 41:29
Psalms 17:8; 52:1–7; 91:1–2; 97:2–3
Isaiah 49:2; 50:10–11
Luke 10:18
Ephesians 2:2; 6:12
1 John 4:3
Revelation 9:1; 14:8; 18:2

RECKLESS
Deuteronomy 32:41
Psalms 11:5; 42:11; 58:4; 140:3
Proverbs 14:16
Matthew 26:52
John 10:10
Romans 12:21
Galatians 5:19–21
1 Peter 5:8
Revelation 12:7–12

Arcana
Genesis 41:8

Proverbs 14:8, 15; 18:2, 7; 28:28
Romans 1:21-23
2 Corinthians 11:12-15
2 Timothy 4:3

cliffside
Genesis 1:1, 6-10, 27
1 Samuel 2:8
Job 9:6; 12:10; 38:4-7, 14
Psalms 75:3; 103:14
Proverbs 8:35-36
Isaiah 40:28; 55:8-9
Matthew 27:5
Acts 1:18-19
Colossians 1:16-17
James 4:14
Revelation 20:15

Pity the soul
Leviticus 19:31
Deuteronomy 6:6-9
Psalms 10:3-4; 75:4; 82:7; 94:4; 115:4-8
John 1:5; 3:19-21; 9:4; 11:10; 12:46
Romans 13:12
Ephesians 6:12

Hinnom
Exodus 23:13; 34:13
Leviticus 18:21
1 Samuel 5:2-7
1 Kings 18:19-40
2 Chronicles 28:1-4
Jeremiah 7:30-34; 19:1-8
Daniel 6:16-24
Matthew 10:28; 25:41

1 Corinthians 10:20-22

hell
Psalms 55:15; 95:7-8
Ecclesiastes 9:10
Isaiah 38:18
Jeremiah 19:6
Hosea 13:14
Joel 2:32
Matthew 3:12; 5:29; 8:12; 13:42; 25:41, 46
Mark 9:48
Luke 10:15; 16:23
John 3:16-20
Romans 10:9, 13; 11:20
2 Corinthians 6:2
Revelation 14:11

Gateway Oceanic
Luke 23:45
Romans 1:19-22
Hebrews 9:1-9, 12; 10:19-20

DESCENT
Genesis 1:2, 26
Job 3:3-6; 27:21-23
Psalms 69:1-2
Luke 19:10
John 10:17-18; 12:46
Romans 10:13
1 Corinthians 15:35-44
Philippians 2:6
James 4:14
1 Peter 2:24

Easter

Psalms 16:10; 22:18; 91:12

Hosea 13:14

Matthew 4:6; 26:6-13, 26; 27:35, 45, 51-54, 59-60, 62-66; 28:6-7

Mark 14:3-9; 15:46; 16:6

Luke 22:19; 23:44-46, 53; 24:6-7, 30-31, 37-43

John 1:14; 2:19; 3:16, 36; 12:1-8; 14:6; 19:32-37; 20:11-19, 25

Acts 2:24; 3:15

Romans 5:9; 6:4-5; 8:38-39

1 Corinthians 8:6; 11:24; 15:55

Ephesians 2:5

Colossians 2:9

1 Thessalonians 1:10

James 2:19

1 Peter 1:18-20

Revelation 7:13-14; 13:8

MESSIAH

Genesis 1:2, 9-10; 2:3; 3:15

Exodus 14:21

Job 1:7

Psalms 91:11-13

Proverbs 16:18

Ecclesiastes 12:6-7

Isaiah 14:12-15; 44:3

Jeremiah 31:33

Jonah 2:1-10

Matthew 8:12; 12:40, 43-45; 14:25; 16:2-4, 21-23; 23:12; 25:41

Luke 4:11; 10:18-19; 19:40

John 4:14; 8:44

Acts 2:24

Romans 10:9

1 Corinthians 2:5; 12:13

2 Peter 2:4

Jude 1:6
Revelation 2:7; 12:4; 13:18; 19:7-9; 20:10; 21:1, 5; 22:1-2

WHO?
Genesis 2:7
Exodus 9:15-16
2 Kings 18:11-12
Psalms 107:29; 139:16
Isaiah 55:11
Jonah 2:10
Matthew 27:51
Mark 4:36-41; 16:3-6
John 1:29; 16:7
Philippians 2:6-11
Hebrews 9:1-9, 12; 10:19-20
Revelation 5:1-6, 12

His Own Accord
Isaiah 53:5
Matthew 26:53; 27:50-51
Luke 24:5-6
John 10:17-18; 14:2; 19:23-24
1 Corinthians 1:18
Colossians 2:15
Hebrews 9:1-9, 12; 10:19-20

Dissolve
Genesis 4:7
Exodus 24:15-17; 34:5
Deuteronomy 21:22-23
Psalms 1:1; 18:11; 97:2
Proverbs 3:7
Matthew 3:2; 21:44; 27:45-50
Luke 22:63-65; 23:35-39
John 1:29

Acts 3:19
Romans 6:8
Galatians 3:13; 5:19-23
2 Timothy 3:2
1 Peter 4:3
1 John 4:8
Revelation 1:7; 5:5-6; 7:10; 19:11-16

A Debt
Psalms 98:9
Proverbs 37:10, 13
Isaiah 53:5
Matthew 10:26-28
Luke 12:2-3
John 3:16
Romans 8:13
2 Corinthians 5:10, 21
Hebrews 9:25-26; 10:14-22
1 Peter 1:14-19; 4:2-5
1 John 4:10
Revelation 20:11-15

The Choice
Isaiah 61:1
Luke 4:18-19; 23:43
1 Corinthians 2:9
2 Corinthians 12:4
Revelation 21:3-4, 25

Inhabited
Genesis 1:1, 14
Job 38:31-33
Psalms 19:1; 139:7
Jeremiah 10:12, 23:24

Dust
Genesis 2:7; 18:27; 28:14
Psalms 103:14
Ecclesiastes 3:20
Isaiah 26:19; 52:7
Daniel 12:2
Romans 10:15

To Return
Joshua 1:9
Proverbs 24:16
1 John 2:1

Sanctifire
Psalms 103:3, 12; 147:16–18
Proverbs 27:17
Isaiah 26:19
Matthew 3:8; 13:31–32; 17:20–21; 26:41
John 6:40
Romans 5:12; 8:1–6
1 Corinthians 3:10–15
James 1:2–4, 14–15
1 Peter 1:3

The Slow Burn
Genesis 2:15
Proverbs 6:6–8; 12:24; 13:4; 20:13
Galatians 6:9
Colossians 3:23
1 Timothy 2:6

Will I?
Psalms 139:16
Proverbs 16:9
Isaiah 25:6

John 2:10
Romans 12:2
1 Corinthians 2:9; 3:12-14
2 Timothy 4:7-8
James 1:12

The Antisceticist
Genesis 1:1-3
Psalms 27:8
Proverbs 7:17, 21-23
Ecclesiastes 1:2; 3:4
Jeremiah 17:9; 29:13
Matthew 7:14; 15:19
John 10:10; 15:11
1 Corinthians 13:12
1 Timothy 4:4
James 1:14-15, 17

Six months only
Job 1:18-21
Psalms 127:3; 137:7-9; 139:13-16
Proverbs 17:17; 27:20
Revelation 9:11

Owen
Genesis 45:4, 14-15
Job 19:13-14
Psalms 127:3; 133:1
Proverbs 17:17
1 John 4:21

stillborn
Genesis 2:24
1 Corinthians 13:4-7
Galatians 5:22-23

Ephesians 5:25, 28
Hebrews 13:4
Revelation 19:7-8; 21:9

A Voice
2 Samuel 22:5-6
Psalms 18:4-5; 34:18; 69:15
1 John 4:11

Still, My God is Good
1 Chronicles 16:34
Job 2:10; 13:15
Psalms 25:8; 33:5; 34:8; 100:4-5; 145:5-7
Mark 10:18
James 1:17
1 John 1:5

Serenity
Psalms 23:2-5
Philippians 4:7
Colossians 2:14; 3:2

The Only Silent Silence
Exodus 33:14
Psalms 91:1
Proverbs 14:30; 127:2
Matthew 6:25-34
Luke 12:25-26
Philippians 4:6-7

Sueño
Psalms 4:8; 127:2
Proverbs 3:24
Ecclesiastes 4:6

Comforter
Psalms 65:8

Monothoughtful
1 Corinthians 13:13; 16:14
Colossians 3:14

HouseHold
Deuteronomy 64:5-6
Psalms 90:1; 91:9
Ephesians 3:16-19
Hebrews 3:6
Revelation 3:20

Withinsanity
John 8:44
1 Corinthians 14:33

"I"
Jeremiah 17:9
Galatians 5:17
James 1:14-15

Emergent, Shattered
Psalms 146:3
Ecclesiastes 6:11; 8:17
Isaiah 31:3
1 Corinthians 8:2

Pinnacle
Genesis 1:26-28
Psalms 8:5-6
1 Corinthians 6:3

Pessoptimism
Genesis 1:31

Psalms 39:4–5; 89:47; 90:4, 10; 102:11
Ecclesiastes 9:4, 7-9; 11:9-10
Isaiah 40:7-8